TINY LIVING SPACES

INNOVATIVE DESIGN SOLUTIONS

LISA BAKER

TINY LIVING SPACES
INNOVATIVE DESIGN SOLUTIONS

BRAUN

TABLE OF CONTENTS

Table of Contents

"MAY YOUR HOME ALWAYS BE TOO SMALL TO HOLD ALL OF YOUR FRIENDS."

Irish proverb

No problem - just move into a Tiny House! However, this rather contradicts the basic idea of the proverb, which wishes the largest possible number of friends. Thus, the quote of the German poet Friedrich Schiller: "The meanest hut hath space to hold a happy loving pair" rather corresponds to the purpose of the Tiny movement. The point of Tiny Houses is to limit oneself in space and thus to concentrate on the essential: on the happy loving pair. All the buildings in this band are sufficient for such a couple, even if some projects also offer space for a happy loving family, while others are designed primarily for self-loving individuals.

Basically, in the Western world, about 30–40 square meters for a single person is considered the "normal" minimum, with at least ten square meters added for each additional person. For four people, this would be 70 square meters, which - in single-story construction with a foundation – would also seal 70 square meters of floor space. The largest Tiny House in this book has an area of 61.3 square meters and has four beds and space for business. The smallest, on the other hand, has only 5.9 square meters, but also does without a kitchen and bathroom, which are shared facilities for several such homes for unhoused citizens. In Germany, in prisons, if the wet room is separated, already nine square meters for two inmates is enough as a decent accommodation, for tenants living in freedom, the same number of square meters is the minimum for one person, according to the Housing Supervision Act. In the first half of the 20th century, when the question of decent housing in crowded cities became urgent, the CIAM (Congrès Internationaux d'Architecture Moderne) demanded 30.5 square meters of living space for a single factory worker: kitchen 14.5 m2 + room 8 m2 + bedroom 8 m2. Ebenezer Howard, author of the *Garden Cities of Tomorrow* (1902) also saw the future of human settlement in small houses surrounded by useable gardens that would contribute to a healthy and self-sufficient lifestyle. Le Corbusier wanted the dwelling to be functionally compressed like a train sleeper - that would mean about 2.40 square meters for one person without and about six square meters for two people with a wet room. Henry David Thoreau, whose book *Walden, or Life in the Woods* (1854) is one of the foundations of the Tiny House movement, allowed himself around 13 square meters (4.57 x 3.05 meters) plus cellar and an externally attached brick fireplace in his wooden hut on foundations in 1845. After all, the author needed a place for the desk. The foundations of the log cabin were excavated in 1945 in the woods of Concord (Massachusetts, USA) at Walden Pond, and today a reconstruction can be visited.

H.D. Thoreau: Walden, or Life in the Woods

In the end there is a difference between sufficient living minimum and sufficient for frugality. On the one hand, the decisive factor is what the occupant can and wants to live without. On the other hand, how cleverly the designer uses the nesting of functions, flexibility of the shell and mobility of individual parts or complete furnishings, but also the given environment has to be considered. Thoreau could not yet come up with such clever solutions, they can be traced back to Le Corbusier's sleeping car analogy: Fold away the bed and put the space to another use. All the buildings shown here are individual designs, which either respond precisely to the needs of known individual users or are aimed at user groups whose behavior and lifestyles have been analyzed. In the case of the latter, the designs become prototypical for series production. A special group are also the non-fixed structures where there is often a blurred transition to the caravan: Here the width is limited by the transport routes, the weight by the tractors. Most of them go somewhere in the nature and the stationary tiny houses are mostly located in exposed places in the landscape, too. Large windows provide a view of magnificent locations: this is not really frugal, however, but rather glamping - glamorous camping. Nevertheless, it is mostly about Thoreau's Life in the woods, less about Howard's digging a vegetable garden, even though the idea of frugality does not only refer to the shelter, but also to the way of living in it. For those who live in a Tiny Home, the salad from the garden is much more appropriate than pizza delivery: only reduction of possessions and consumption makes the simple life intended.

Of course, simplicity in one's lifestyle is not something you would just switch to overnight. For this very reason, there are more and more Tiny Homes that propose temporary habitation: as personal or rentable vacation homes. Such houses for valuable leisure time should then of course be located in idyllic places and in the sense of a minimal impact on nature is tiny then also sustainable. Basically, however, tiny houses are not sustainable per se. They would not have to be built with environmentally friendly materials, nor would they, by definition, seal little ground. In the case of multi-story buildings - a skyscraper of Tiny Homes - the degree of sealing per occupant naturally remains significantly lower. In many of the examples in this book, you can also see at first glance that the designers have also thought about this by keeping the sealing as low as possible. And finally, the enjoyment of nature is a major trigger for the desire to preserve it. Or, as Thoreau wrote on the title page of his book: "I do not propose to write an ode to dejection, but to brag as lustily as chanticleer in the morning, standing on his roost, if only to wake my neighbors up."

THE HIVE AUSTIN

Design:
Nicole Blair

Location:
Austin, Texas, USA

Job:
Build a guest house behind a primary residence

Client:
Kerthy Fix

GFA:
51 m2

Completion:
2015

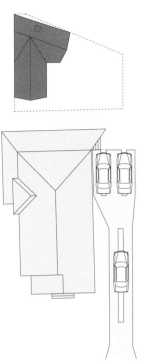

Site plan

Ground and second floor plan

The Hive Austin

Tiny Living Spaces

The Hive's 30-square-meter footprint is the maximum allowed on this residential lot to not exceed the City of Austin's impervious cover requirement. To gain enough area to fit a one-bedroom dwelling, walls tilt from the slab, hugging building setback planes and an angled utility easement at the back of the property, to add volume where needed — evoking the shape of a beehive. By carefully tailoring the space in three dimensions, rooms are cut down and expanded to suit the program. While the box form is the reigning standard for economy of construction, inefficiencies can emerge when examining other factors like material excess, energy consumption and oversizing. Like a well designed garment, a building may perform best when tailored to the shape and movement of its inhabitants.

THE ORCHID TINY HOME

Design:
David Latimer and New Frontier Design

Location:
Southern California, USA

Job:
Build a Scandinavian inspired tiny home

Client:
Confidential

GFA:
20.8 m2

Completion:
2019

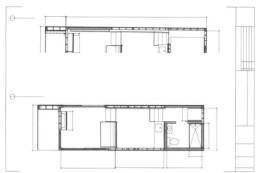

Ground floor and loft plan

The tiny house was inspired by the solar eclipse of 2017. It comes alive at night through LED strip lights in the interior and exterior that are covered by valence pieces of cedar and maple trim. Like a full solar eclipse, the valances hide the source of the light itself, create a sharp crisp line, and turn the maple plywood walls into a source of light. The asymmetrical shape, eaveless gable roof, and cantilevered deck give the home a Scandinavian aesthetic. The contrast of this contemporary minimalist style is juxtaposed with the cedar exterior cladding that gives a warmth to the shape. The cedar cladding is raised 4 centimeters off of the walls and roof which give a floating effect. Natural light, a glass garage door, a pull out sofa-bed, hidden storage, a loft with a king size bed, and a walk-in closet make this space feel larger than it is.

WOODNEST

Design:
Helen & Hard Architects

Location:
Odda, Norway

Job:
Create an unique spatial experience that
connects climbing and exploring trees

Client:
Sally and Kjartan Aano

GFA:
15 m2

Completion:
2020

Inextricably crafted from nature, each treehouse is suspended five to six meters above the forest floor and fastened with a steel collar to the individual trunk of a living pine tree. At just 15 sqaure meters, carefully organised inside around the central tree trunk itself are four sleeping places, a bathroom, a kitchen area and a living space. Inspired by the Norwegian cultural traditions of vernacular timber architecture, together with a desire to experiment with the material potential of wood, the architecture is structurally supported by the tree trunk itself, and formed from a series of radial glu-laminated timber ribs. The untreated natural timber shingles encase the volume creating a protective skin around the building, which will weather over time to merge and blend with the natural patina of the surrounding forest.

Tiny Living Spaces

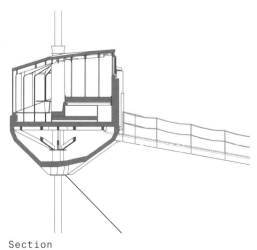

Section

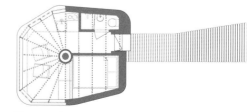

Floor plan

Woodnest

CHANDLER BOULEVARD TINY HOME VILLAGE

Design:
Lehrer Architects

Location:
Los Angeles, California, USA

Job:
Build a tiny home village for unhoused citizens

Client:
City of Los Angeles

GFA:
5.9 m2

Completion:
2021

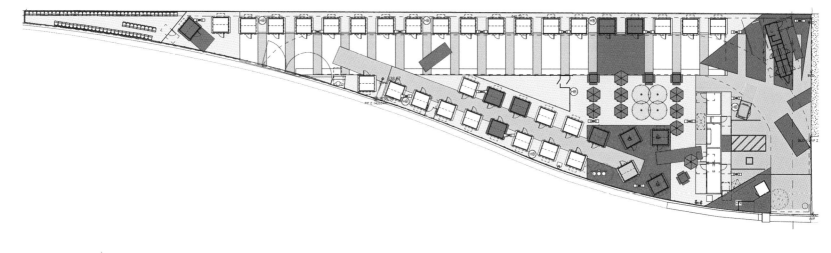

Site plan

The village is an innovative community project offering an aggressive, experimental and timely template for improving Los Angeles' homelessness crisis. It turned a forgotten infill lot into a facility for homeless Angelenos. A humane and welcoming environment was created with the chosen design meant to uplift residents and enhance the neighborhood. Because such projects often face opposition from neighbors, a place of significance that blends into the neighborhood can help combat preconceived notions about homeless shelters.Low cost details like modernist paint highlights were chosen to create variety, delight and sense of community. The project consists of prefabricated modular units. Beside the houses, a dining and gathering space and other services and social buildings were added.

Chandler Boulevard Tiny Home Village

MOOBLE
HOUSE

Design:
Mooble House

Location:
Podbanské, Slovakia

Job:
Provide mobile and modular living solutions

Client:
Confidential

GFA:
17.2 m2

Completion:
2022

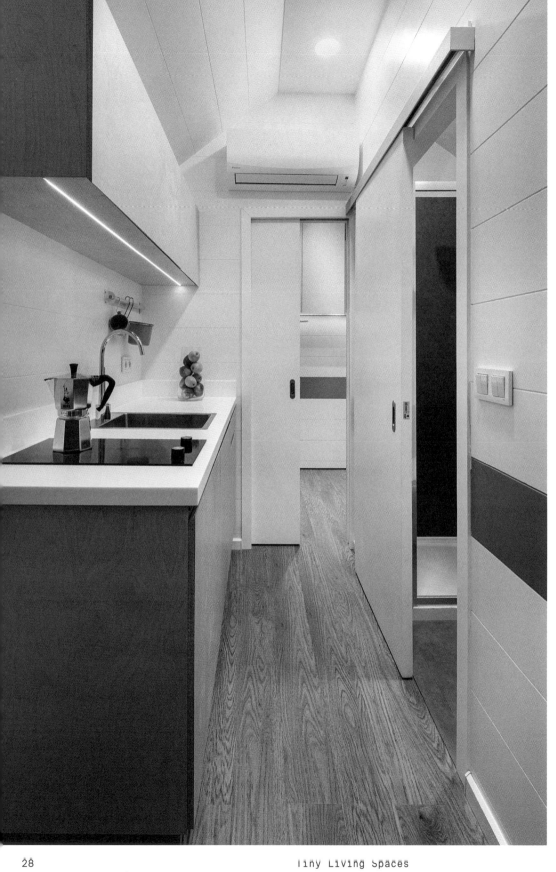
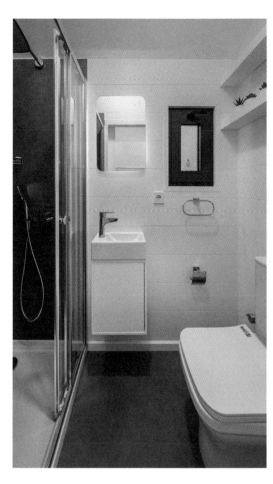

Floor plan

Mooble House

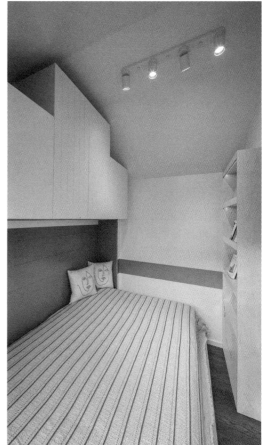

Mooble House allows the users experience any location in home comfort. Mooble House Mo.2 675 S is a tiny house model in which sleeping and living areas are designed as separate spaces. The continuity of the furniture and its ability to transform into different functions are adopted in the design philosophy. The folding wall bed in the sleeping area creates a new space for various purposes when closed. The furniture, which is used as a fixed desk in the living area, also contains storage areas and turns into a dining table. Equipping road legal tiny houses with functional furnitures, Mooble House redefines the relation between weight, design, comfort and functionality in a minimal space in combination of expertise in various design and engineering disciplines.

CIRCULAR TINY HOUSE

Design:
Rainer Hirth, Anders Macht,
Christopher Nguyen, Til-Oliver Frank et. al.

Location:
Coburg, Germany

Job:
Research on building sustainable

Client:
School of Design – Coburg University

GFA:
19 m2

Completion:
2022

The project goal was an energy self-sufficient, space-optimized and environmentally friendly tiny house built from renewable materials. By optimizing the space, the building was created cost-effectively, but is still architecturally sophisticated. Building materials whose production generates greenhouse gases and a lot of energy were avoided. Sustainable and regional building materials were used, especially straw and clay. In addition, care was taken to avoid long transport routes. By applying the cradle-to-cradle principle, used and reused components were applied wherever possible. Thanks to photovoltaics, the house is self-sufficient in terms of energy and can be used as a guest house for the faculty.

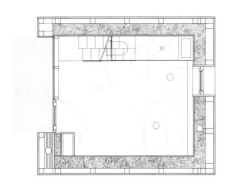

Floor plan

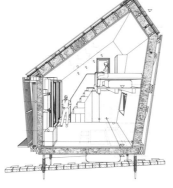

Section

Circular Tiny House

GLAMBOX PROJECT

Design:
Studio Officina82

Location:
Garessio, Italy

Job:
Make a cabin to enjoy the sky

Client:
Selucente snc

GFA:
22 m2

Completion:
2021

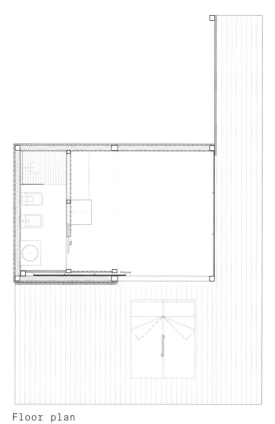

Floor plan

Tiny Living Spaces

GlamBOX is inspired by the haylofts of the surroundings, an inevitable presence in Alpine rural areas part of a consolidated landscape image. The five by three meter chestnut wood module is organized on two levels: on the ground floor there are a bedroom and bathroom, on the mezzanine there are two more potential beds for children. The roofing is made of a Corten steel sheet. The external chestnut tables are dark obtained thanks to the traditional Japanese technique known as Shou Sugi Ban which involves a treatment with fire to protect the wooden surfaces from atmospheric events. The external wooden platform is placed at the same level as the floor and allows the bed, mounted on a trolley, to slide out to enjoy the outdoor space and the sky while lying down.

TREEH BIOSPHERE

Design:
Bjarke Ingels Group

Location:
Harads, Sweden

Job:
Create a tree house benefiting the environment

Client:
Treehotel

GFA:
34 m2

Completion:
2022

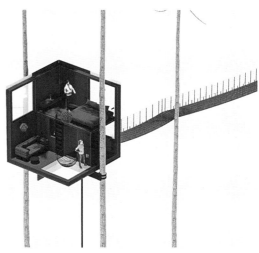

Interior model

The tree house designed by BIG together with ornithologist Ulf Öhman brings 350 bird houses with it. With that, they seek to enhance the surrounding biosphere. The aim is to decrease the downward spiral of the bird population in the Swedish woods and instead strengthen the biosphere and natural habitat. The Treeh Biosphere is accessed via a suspended bridge that slopes from the ground to the top of the trees. The interior incorporates rich dark interiors and organic materials inspired by the surrounding landscape, which further serve to reinforce the visitors' gaze outwards and to focus on the natural beauty of the surroundings. Additionally, the roof terrace – close to the treetop canopies – offers a 360-degree view of the forest.

TOCHKA NA KARTE

Design:
Rhizome

Location:
Vidlitsa, Repulic of Karelia, Russia

Job:
Build 15 holiday homes in an untouched forest

Client:
Country hotel Tochka na Karte

GFA:
37 m2

Completion:
2020

Vidlitsa Country Hotel lays isolated and is surrounded by wild Karelian landscape. The core of the hotel is formed by 15 bijou private houses with panoramic glazing and individual terraces that provide a personal view to nature. All of the houses are built with the usage of prefabricated technology. Every cabin consists of two modules making up the L-shaped area, including a large terrace, a compact space capable of accommodating up to four guests and a personal sauna. Diverse architectural environment is realized through four exterior design types and each house stands out with the textures of façades that vary from smooth to ribbed surfaces. Impregnated pine wood was chosen as a finishing material and every type is also complimented with specific variation of canopies.

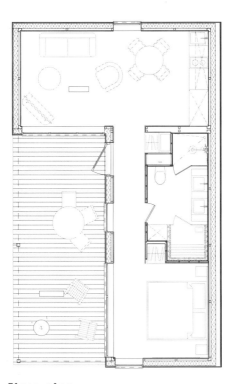

Floor plan

Tochka na Karte

THE PERCH

Design:
Nicole Blair

Location:
Austin, Texas, USA

Job:
Provide a studio above a primary residence

Client:
Dylan Robertson and Annie Cobb

GFA:
61.3 m2

Completion:
2021

Tiny Living Spaces

Floor plan

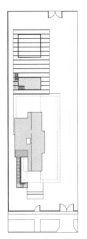

Site plan

The Perch

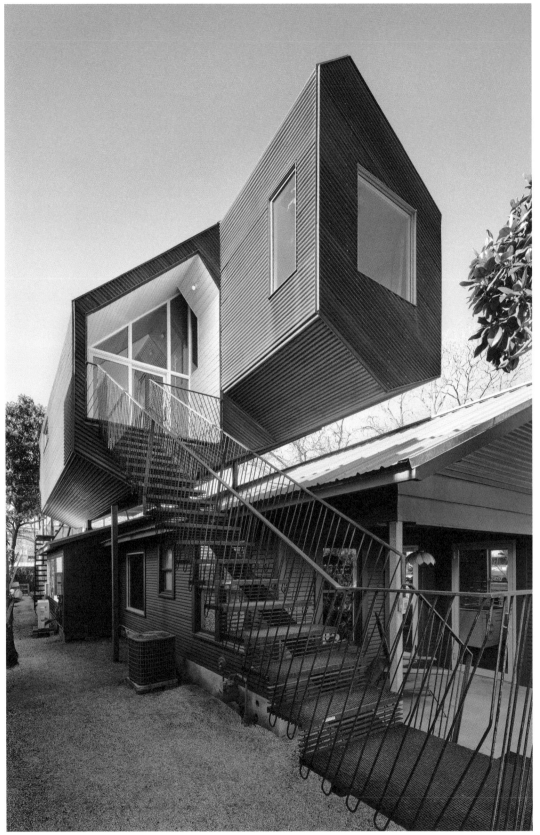

Tiny Living Spaces

The Perch is shaped to fit just above the existing bungalow roofline and just below the City of Austin setback tent. Rooms have small footprints and vaulted ceilings for added volume, and the split-level form provides interstitial storage and mechanical space throughout. Structural steel throughout is left exposed and painted white. A hard-working beam in the kitchen supports an open shelf above the kitchen sink, carries the bedroom floor behind, allows the kitchen countertop to extend deep beyond the sink for added storage. Materials were selected for economy, durability, and efficiency, including off-the-shelf pre-finished pine walls and ceilings, off-the-shelf butcher block countertops, cabinets and standard porcelain sockets and pendant lights the client already owned.

CABIN ONE

Design:
Home One

Location:
Groß Nemerow, Germany

Job:
Build a vacation home with a panoramic view

Client:
Auszeit Tollensesee

GFA:
35 m2

Completion:
2022

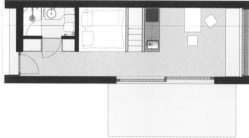

Floor plan

Cabin One is a serial prefabricated house, where special attention was paid to durability and quality. The small space accommodates all the features for a functional house so that residents do not have to sacrifice comfort. The placement and size of the windows are purposefully designed to flood the rooms with lots of natural sunlight. Natural materials such as oak wood allow for the most sustainable living in harmony with the environment. The black kitchen furniture and details in this tiny home create an impressive contrast to the natural wood paneling. Electricity can be generated by solar energy. The interior design approach focuses strongly on spatial quality and functionality.

HALF-TREE HOUSE

Design:
Jacobschang Architecture

Location:
Barryville, New York, USA

Job:
Build a single-room cabin in the forest
for contemplation

Client:
Confidential

GFA:
34 m2

Completion:
2016

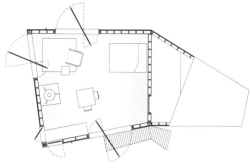

Floor plan

The Half-Tree House offers everything you need and is located on a privately owned second-growth forest. True to its name, the tiny house is lifted above the ground and relies upon support from the trees. The black exterior façade clearly contrasts with the white interior walls and both were milled and kiln dried from the Eastern Pines felled on the property. The floor-to-ceiling windows and glass doors allow visitors to observe precipitation or wild animals in peace while sheltered inside. And although much of the façade has been glazed, visitors are protected from too much sunlight by the forest's surrounding trees. But there is still enough light coming in to spend time there. The space is heated with a highly efficient Jotul wood stove and power, if needed, is drawn from a portable generator.

LUMIPOD

Design:
Lumicene

Location:
Volvic, France

Job:
Build a minimalistic house immersed in nature

Client:
Confidential

GFA:
18 m2

Completion:
2021

LumiPod is a prefabricated housing module characterized by a minimalistic design organized around a unique curved glass window. It is installed in Volvic, France, with a view to the Chaîne des Puys volcanoes. The curved glass is framed with aluminum and slides between two rails, allowing the interior space to be smoothly transformed into an outdoor space. The bedroom therefore can be used as a traditional bedroom and can also be used as a semi-open space towards nature. LumiPod eliminates the boundary between interior and exterior to make way for an unforgettable experience. It is meant to be a refuge to city dwellers seeking relief in nature. Within 18 square meters, it offers a bedroom, a shower area, a toilet and a wardrobe.

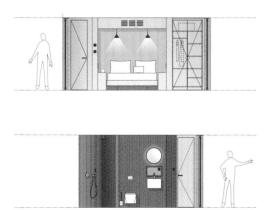

Bath area and bedroom

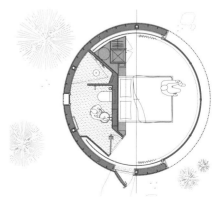

Ground floor

LumiPod

CABIN Y

Design:
dmvA

Location:
Anywhere

Job:
Develop a sustainable and custom-made
mobile unit

Client:
Confidential

GFA:
12 m2

Completion:
2019

Cabin Y consists of a beam-shaped volume with a footprint of six by 2.4 meters and a height of 3.4 meters. The goal was to make the cabin as light as possible to transport it easily. The cabin consists of ten wooden porches that are connected by stainless steel tension cables in an X-shape, whereby the compressive forces are neutralized when being lifted with a crane. Cabin Y has a thermal insulation with hemp fibers installed. The exterior consists of burnt larch wood and for the interior white oiled pine was used. Burning wood is a natural way to make wood durable. The unit is equipped with a toilet, a shower, and duplex sleeping accommodation. Solar panels on the roof provide the cabin with energy. The front façade is entirely in glass with a steel frame as pivoting door. The whole cabin is custom-made.

Tiny Living Spaces

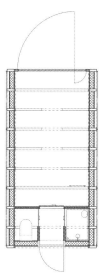

Floor plan

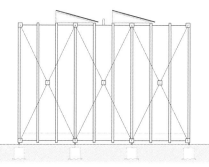

Elevation

69

Cabin Y

TINY HOUSE MAVEA

Design:
Kms Tinyhouse Manufaktur

Location:
Steinmauern, Germany

Job:
Make a tiny house with a view to the stars

Client:
Confidential

GFA:
33.5 m2

Completion:
2021

Ground floor plan

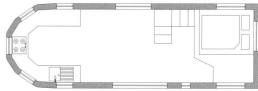

First floor plan

It was a focus of the architects to create a tiny living space in harmony with nature. The characteristic curves together with clear lines give a feeling of security, and at the same time harmonize with nature in the surrounding area. The high ceiling makes the tiny house seem more spacious. The house is equipped with a kitchen and a bath, including a standard sized shower and storage space. Above the bathroom is the open bedroom with a skylight window. The house was built with a focus on sustainable design and regenerating materials. Wooden post and beam construction with sheep wool insulation and the façade and windows made of wood give the house a pleasant living climate. The flat roof can be greened and the house can be moved since it is not installed permanently on the ground.

NILIAITTA — KIVIJÄRVI RESORT

Design:
Studio Puisto Architects

Location:
Kivijärvi, Finland

Job:
Raise a structure in an national park

Client:
Municipality of Kivijärvi

GFA:
36 m2

Completion:
2020

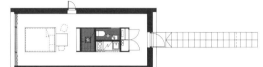

Floor plan

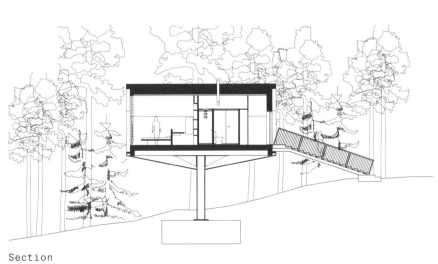

Section

Niliaitta - Kivijärvi Resort

Tiny Living Spaces

The site for Kivijärvi Resort is located in a unique region of Finland near Salamajärvi National Park with both rich natural biodiversity and a need for ecologically sensitive solutions to support nature tourists accustomed to high-quality accommodation. The overall structure is raised on a single pillar to maintain only minimal contact with the nature below, and after construction, the forest terrain below has been restored to its original appearance. Similarly, the cabin itself was strategically positioned so that only a few trees needed to be taken down during construction and only a narrow path grants acces. To remain environmentally sensitive, the materials of the Niliaitta prototype are all ecological with the use of wood in all interior surfaces, eco-wool as insulation, and the avoidance of plastic in the structures.

CRUACHAN BEAG

Design:
BARD

Location:
Coilleag, Isle of Eriskay, United Kingdom

Job:
Refurbish and repurpose a stone ruin

Client:
Andy Laverty and family

GFA:
30 m2

Completion:
2020

Floor plan

The project utilized an existing stone ruin, to form a space to dine, to rest and to bathe, whilst maximizing the beautiful outlook. It was considered from the outset how the building could be designed to improve with the actions of time. An entrance sequence containing a number of 90-degree turns was the initial design generator. A small area of the ruin is left open and building-free, creating a sheltered court to form an entrance, and a place to sit, store logs, and decompress from the outside world. From here the first turn leads to the stove, followed by a diagonal to the view. The building is firmly rooted in its site. The sense of space and outlook to the scottish coast opens the tiny house up and makes it seem spacious. It is now another onlooker to its immense surroundings with a renewed purpose.

Cruachan Beag

SUSPENDED VILLA

Design:
Ev Design Office

Location:
Deylaman, Guilan, Iran

Job:
Raise a new tiny house from the ground

Client:
Mr. Hashemi

GFA:
45 m2

Completion:
2022

Exploded drawing

Despite the small size of the project, Suspended Villa has countable practical and suitable spaces. The presence of a large balcony in this project allows users to spend more time in the nature and in the house itself at the same time. This project is located in Deylaman, Guilan. A mountainous area, surrounded by trees and green lands. The Suspended Villa is lifted up from the ground by the help of a concrete base, as if the project is also part of the forest itself, and in order to affect the nature around the site as little as possible. Large balconies, lifting the building up from the ground, the use of sloping roof and wood in the interior design of the project is taken out from the traditional methods of architecture in Guilan.

TINY HOUSE MORITZ

Design:
Tiny Homeland

Location:
Worpswede, Germany

Job:
Build a tiny home for vacation

Client:
Land of Green

GFA:
38 m2

Completion:
2021

Floor plan

The tiny house Moritz is a home for vacationers. Despite the name, the tiny house is not so tiny, thanks to an expendable slider the first floor is 36 square meters. The house was named after the German author and theater writer Moritz Rinke. The name links the house to its location, since Rinke grew up in the same place where the Tiny House Moritz is located today: Worpswede, a small town in Northern Germany and famous former artists community. The house can accommodate up to five adults, has five sleeping places and offers a fully equipped bathroom and kitchen. The interior is modern and the mix of natural timber floors and details as well as black and white furniture gives it an elegant look.

THE HERMITAGE

Design:
llabb architettura

Location:
Val Trebbia, Italy

Job:
Provide a small multi-functional guest room

Client:
Private

GFA:
12 m2

Completion:
2021

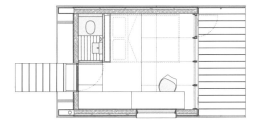

Floor plan

Tiny Living Spaces

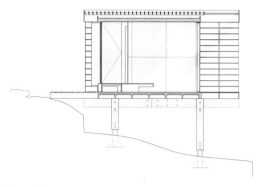

Elevation

The Hermitage

Tiny Living Spaces

The Hermitage is a space of contemplation and reflection. Isolated from the world, it overlooks a still wild valley, secluded from everything. This is defined by wood panels, vertical and horizontal lines that are tuned in a thin yet clear equilibrium. The artefact is a hybridisation between a Japanese tea house and a Scandinavian cabin. It seems to recall the use of materials typically used in architecture, like metal façades and beam structures, reinterpreted through the use of wood. The walls, floor, and ceiling have been pre-assembled and are composed of Okoumè marine plywood panels, a wood chosen for its resistance to weathering. The project was realized in two weeks, in order to deepen compositional themes and to transmit the "design with your hands" that characterizes the llabb architettura work.

KNAPPHULLET

Design:
Lundhagem

Location:
Sandefjord, Norway

Job:
Design a small house next to a holiday home

Client:
Karine Denizou, Svein Lund

GFA:
30 m2

Completion:
2014

Knapphullet is a seperate addition to a family holiday home. The space expands vertically over three levels including a roof terrace. The bed is lifted to get a better view, making the rest of the space more useable. The house is situated between large rocks surrounded by low vegetation. The project started with an idea of how to utilize this naturally sheltered area. The idea developed to create a way to climb up from this shelter to see the panoramic view which led to the shape of the roof: A stepped ramp leads up from the terrain, connects to the landscape beyond. The interior walls are solid oak layered with a natural sawn texture, while the acoustic ceiling is covered with woven oak strips. The long bench is made with the same white concrete as the roof tying both inside and outside spaces together.

Situation

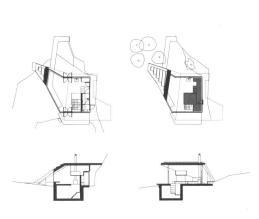

Floor plans and sections

Knapphullet

TOPOL 27

Design:
DublDom

Location:
Kaluga Oblast, Russia

Job:
Create a home for instant moving-in

Client:
DublDom

GFA:
27 m2

Completion:
2021

Topol 27 has a bedroom, kitchen, living room, bathroom and dressing room – a maximum of comfortable space on a minimum area. The set includes furniture, kitchen, curtains, dishes, cutlery, household appliances, outdoor and indoor lamps, and a terrace. Most of the interior items are selected in chain stores, so that they can be quickly replaced, which is important for the rental business. The project uses eco-friendly and wear-resistant materials suitable for active use in daily rental conditions. Natural oak is combined with black metal, stone kitchen countertops, and glass. On the floor is a wear-resistant and hypoallergenic material. A large amount of glass harmoniously connects the interior and the natural environment.

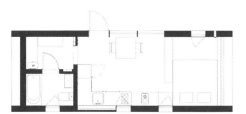

Floor plan

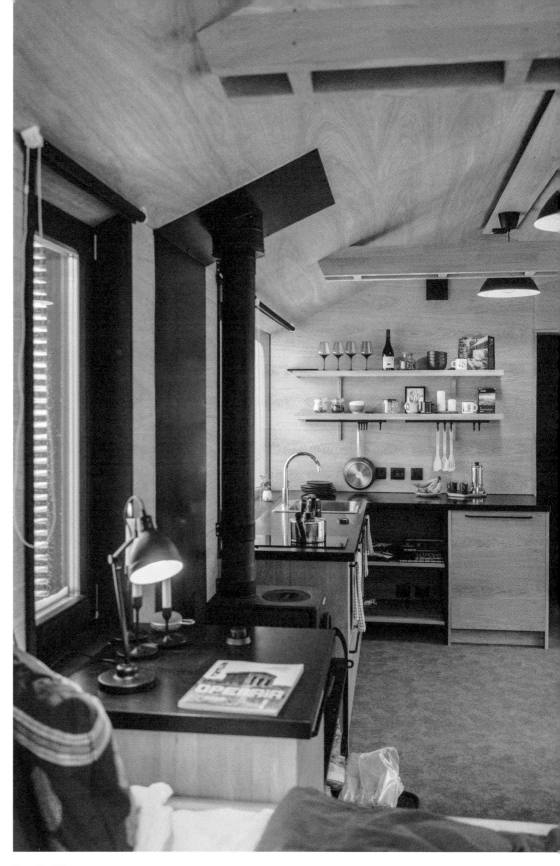

MELIDES
TREE
HOUSE

Design:
Madeiguincho Atelier

Location:
Alentejo, Portugal

Job:
Design a tree house on a plain of pines and cork oaks

Client:
Confidential

GFA:
25 m2

Completion:
2019

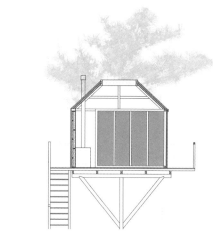

Longitudinal section with stairs

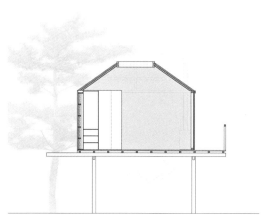

Cross section

Melides Tree House

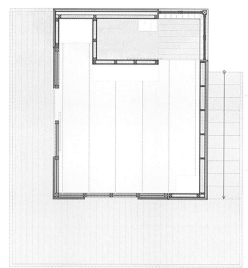

Floor plan

The tree house was built on a plain of pines and cork oaks. The architects chose a young and healthy pine on a plateau overlooking the Atlantic Ocean. The aim was that the pine would serve as protection for the house and that the project would embrace the tree. Thus, it became natural to choose the material inspired by the surroundings. The raw materiality and simplicity of the spatial experience makes the distance more palpable from an urban way of life. In this way, it made sense to allow the evolution of this concept to the outside, through a balcony and with a view of the sea. The bathroom of this shelter reminds its user of its relationship with nature, from all the water circuits used, to the breeze, overlooking the pine forest, without compromising comfort.

ESTÚDIO ELO

Design:
Ticiane Lima

Location:
São Paulo, Brazil

Job:
Design a sustainable tiny house with everything essential for a human being to live

Client:
CasaCor exhibition of architecture

GFA:
14.4 m2

Completion:
2020

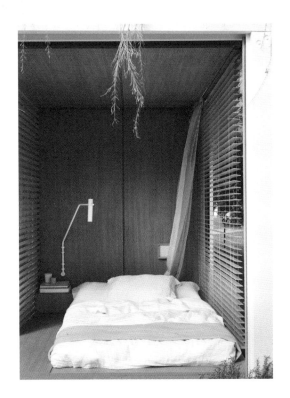

Estúdio Elo, inspired by works of art to present the house of 'the new living', is a project inside a container. The environment is totally compact, divided into kitchen, office, bath, bedroom and rooftop, with Scandinavian design, sustainable light wood, natural materials, little furniture and multifunctional spaces, bringing the concept and awareness of what is really essential for human beings to live with quality of life. The project is inspired by the work of Ricardo Bueno, whose concept unites brass and blown glass in a single piece. The architect proposes an analogy between the work of art and the new home, where the delicate space of the crystal represents our home, in a moment of adversity and transitions, which is at the same time a sensitive and supportive place.

Floor plan

Estúdio Elo

RAUS X SIGURD LARSEN

Design:
Raus and Sigurd Larsen Architekten

Location:
Schlossgarten, Berlin area, Germany

Job:
Build a cabin that seamlessly blends into nature

Client:
Stay Raus GmbH

GFA:
17 m2

Completion:
2022

Floor plan

Raus is a platform for nature immersion. With its smart and carefully designed cabins, the Berlin-based company offers retreats at unique locations in the midst of nature. The cabin model, designed by architect Sigurd Larsen, is inspired by the idea of framing idyllic views and making tiny space appear bigger than it is. The dark interior allows for an unbroken view of nature, as it barely creates any reflections in the glass. Bed, sofa, bunk bed and bathroom come as small niches in a wall and the front of the cabin is equipped with high ceilings and large sliding doors. But not only the big windows ensure an extraordinary view. As a special feature of the design, the skylights in the bathroom and above the bunk bed allow you to gaze up into the crown of the tree above.

IN PRAISE OF SHADOWS — WRITERS' CABIN

Design:
Rintala Eggertsson Architects

Location:
Vaud, Switzerland

Job:
Build an inspiring cabin for writers and authors

Client:
Fondation Jan Michalski

GFA:
55.6 m2

Completion:
2017

Tiny Living Spaces

In Praise Of Shadows - Writers' Cabin

The In Praise Of Shadows cabin resembles the cross in the Swiss coat of arms, which connects the concepts of divinity and the world through the union of the vertical and the horizontal. The walls of the cabin are composed of three layers of insulation set inside a structural steel frame. Also, the surface materials of the cabin are entirely wooden products. This helps the independent structure in hanging from the big canopy by making it as light as possible. Although the interior of the cabin is divided into four levels, they still maintain a large degree of interconnectivity due to the fact that they are set on half-levels to each other. The water and heating central can be located on the lowest level close to the toilet and the kitchen, next to the entrance and the staircase which can serve as a duct for water pipes and electric cables.

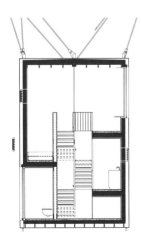

Floor plan

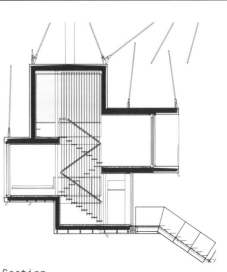

Section

In Praise Of Shadows - Writers' Cabin

OBSERVATORY TINY HOUSE

Design:
MNDA studio

Location:
Lodi Italy

Job:
Find a new way of experiencing smart work in the pandemic era

Client:
Confidential

GFA:
56 m2

Completion:
2020

Tiny Living Spaces

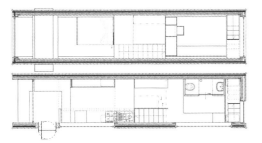

Ground and upper floor plan

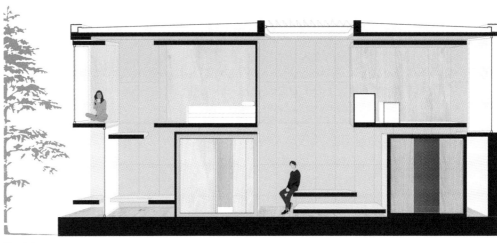

Section

The project derives from the search for a better quality of life in the pandemic era, enhancing the simplicity of life with respect for nature using ecological and natural systems. The Observatory Tiny House was conceived from two prefabricated containers, superimposed on each other and reworked. Multiple glass façades got implemented to supply the entire house with natural light. The house is designed to offer simple and versatile living comfort with the possibility of moving to different natural areas of the world and being able to face different climates with a highly eco-friendly structure. The interior spaces offer a work station and both horizontal and vertical astronomical observation points, for greater contact with nature and the surrounding space. The Observatory displays a game of volumes between full and empty.

Observatory Tiny House

CASA PROA

Design:
Atelier Marko Brajovic

Location:
Paraty, Rio de Janeiro, Brazil

Job:
Design a tiny tree house by triangular modulations

Client:
Maria Christina de Andrade

GFA:
30 m2

Completion:
2021

Isometric drawing

Triangulation is the essence of natural special organisation of forces in dynamic equilibrium. The tetrahedron, explored widely by Richard Buckminster Fuller, is the most stable and space-filling structure, in fact nature's basic simplest structural system. Casa Proa (Bow House in Portuguese) was designed with triangular modulations on different scales. An equilateral triangular volume was installed at Praia do Rosa beach, located between a Mango tree, the traditional colonial house, and a major rock, on steep waterfront terrain. From structure, to floor plan, from roof system to custom furniture and finishings the triangular geometry modulates everything and creates a visual pattern. The main sleeping room is in the center, behind it the kitchen and on side triangles the entrance and opposite a bathroom.

Casa Proa

CABIN ANNA

Design:
ANNA

Location:
Wildlife reserve De Biesbosch, The Netherlands

Job:
Design a futuristic tiny house using glass
and wood

Client:
Confidential

GFA:
30 m2

Completion:
2022

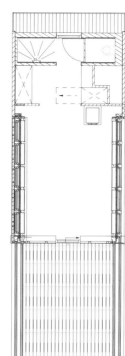

Floor plan

Cabin Anna

Anna Stay Model 2022 is not a cabin but a spaceship that brings you back to Planet Earth. It has two protective sliding shells that allow to open up and become part of the surroundings. The inner shell is made of double glass, the outer shell is made of wood. By adjusting the two shells Anna changes and adapts to the weather, the users mood, or the occasion. Anna allows to connect to a reality in which we naturally belong. Because Anna, just like any other organism, responds to the environment and moves with the rhythm of nature, inhabitants become part of it instead of being merely a spectator. This way one can experience the beauty of a fierce rain shower from under the glass roof, and wake up among the birds in the early morning, mesmerize at night by the starry sky directly above the bed.

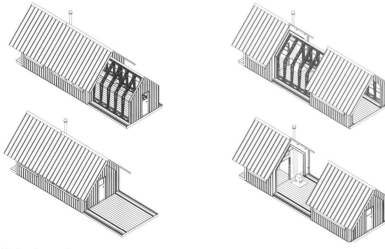

Main layouts

Cabin Anna

MICRO HOME IN WARSAW

Design:
DESEA Architects and Adam Pszczółkowski

Location:
Warsaw, Poland

Job:
Make a small house for family recreation

Client:
Adam Pszczółkowski

GFA:
35 m2

Completion:
2018

The tiny house is located in the city area of Warsaw. It is part of the recreation plot, an open green space in the middle of the city. The house has two pass-through entrances, which open it towards the natural surroundings. The two side glazings on front and back give the house a transparent flair. The front elevation is equipped with a wooden bench alongside the whole length of the building. It is hidden underneath the roofing above and creates a space to rest with a view at nature. The façades consist of HPL panels (high-quality laminated panels) and waterproof plywood. Both the main and side entrance doors were handmade. The furniture consists of a line of white kitchen cabinets suspended above the floor.

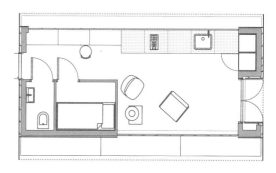

Floor plan

Micro Home in Warsaw

PERMANENT CAMPING 2

Design:
Rob Brown and Antje Mahler

Location:
Berry, Australia

Job:
Distille the demands of living to the essentials

Client:
Confidential

GFA:
18 m2

Completion:
2020

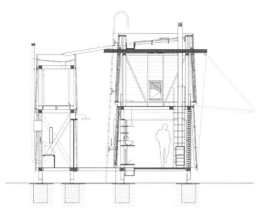

Section

Permanent Camping 2

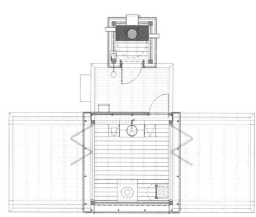

Floor plan

Overlooking the Pacific Ocean amongst lush green paddocks stand two tiny copper towers providing the essential requirements for shelter. The structure is made from recycled iron bark, sourced from an unused wharf float. For this construction the architects worked with the builders from Smith and Primmer and the craftsman Jeffrey Broadfield. The interior walls are clad in wood. The ground level includes facilities to cook, store things and heat the cabin. The bed is accessed via a ladder. The bathroom is a separate tower with its own water tank storing rainwater. A ladder provides access to the roof. A getaway, a permanent tent, a place to enjoy nature, and live simply. The cabin is accessible only by foot. It can be seen from a distance in the landscape presenting itself as a small sculpture.

BRETTE HAUS RUSTIC

Design:
Brette Haus

Location:
Hollenbek, Germany

Job:
Invent a foldable house installation in a
railroad cart

Client:
Erlebnisbahn Ratzeburg GmbH

GFA:
20 m2

Completion:
2021

Building stages

Unpacking after transport

The Rustic foldable house consists of three parts – the main, engineering, and roof modules. The main module serves as a living room. The engineering part contains a WC, bathroom, and kitchen. The space under the roof serves as the mezzanine bedroom or storage area. Altogether it folds into a compact-size module for transport. Inside the folded cabin, all space is rationally used to store additional panels and sealing elements of the building. The process of unfolding and installing the house is quite simple and takes only three hours. The core materials which provide the ultimate sustainability of the building are cross-laminated timber (CLT) and wood-fiber insulation. Natural materials increase a healthy environment and create a comfortable microclimate inside the house.

CABANA

Design:
Liga Arquitetura e Urbanismo

Location:
Serra do Cipó, Brazil

Job:
Build a sustainable cabin in a national park

Client:
Tiago Abdo

GFA:
33 m2

Completion:
2021

The Cabana was designed in such a way that it can be adapted to any ground and location, while trying to reduce the environmental impact. This was achieved by the choice of materials and the time of implantation. The Cabana has a fully modular metallic structure and uses rockwool for insulation. It also uses large PVC frames, which are positioned in order to favor cross ventilation. The goal was to reduce the need to use air conditioning systems and artificial lighting, to consequently minimize the consumption of electricity. The ground floor consists of a living room and a small kitchen. In addition, there also is the bath with tropical plants in the back of the ground floor. The mezzanine provides a bed and a hanger area. It also gains a lot of privacy by using the wall above the kitchen as cover.

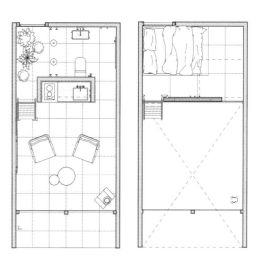

Ground and first floor plan

Cabana

WIKKELHOUSE

Design:
Wikkelhouse

Location:
The Netherlands

Job:
Create a sustainable modular house

Client:
Confidential

GFA:
5.52 m2 each segment

Completion:
2021

Wikkelhouse is a unique modular concept for a home, creative space, or office. It is produced sustainable. The base of Wikkelhouse is virgin fiber paperboard. This is wrapped around a house-shaped mold while eco-friendly glue is added, creating a tough and insulating sandwich structure. By this wrapping process a heat insulation and construction method is integrated in a sustainable way. The cardboard is wrapped in breathable foil to make it waterproof. The basic construction consists of 1.2 meter deep interlocking segments to extend or shorten the length of the house. Due to its low weight of 500 kilos per segment, Wikkelhouse does not need a foundation. This makes it possible to move the house to another location. The segments can be reused and are fully recyclable.

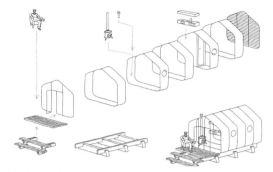

Schematic drawing

Wikkelhouse

MUMA HUT

Design:
WeWilder Studio and Miodrag Stoianov

Location:
Sat-Bătrân, Romania

Job:
Build a suspended room in the orchard

Client:
Daniel Hurduzeu

GFA:
15 m2

Completion:
2021

MuMA Hut is a tiny house built with voluntaries in an orchard, inviting guests who want to experience nature with an audacious window onto the landscape. It came to life through a workshop over several weekends. The wood was purchased from the area to revitalize traditional practices. Also some material was manufactured in the region, since a local craftsman made the shingles. The idea was sparked by Danu, a local ranger who wanted to make his childhood tree house come back to life and was set in motion when architect Miodrag Stoianov offered his support to the WWF initiative in the area, where more than 120 bison roam freely in nature. The hut is also a prototype for the WeWilder Campus, a set of cottages and a co-working space in nature, opened in September 2022.

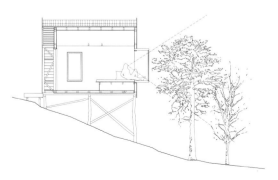

Longitudinal section

Front and back

MuMA Hut

LUNA TINY HOME

Design:
David Latimer and New Frontier Design

Location:
San Juan Islands, Washington, USA

Job:
Build an efficient, affordable luxury home

Client:
Confidential

GFA:
18.1 m2

Completion:
2021

Tiny Living Spaces

Floor plan

Luna Tiny Home

The shape of the Luna Tiny Home mimics the mountains it is inspired by. The interior has a warm and cozy palette of colors and materials. Clean, all-white shiplap cladding, and white-washed reclaimed wood flooring create a textured, bright space. Pops of walnut, black, and green plants add a color and texture. Though tiny, the kitchen is equipped with a dishwasher, and a washer/dryer combo unit. The staircase rises up to the loft, where a king-size bed perches. The large glass window wall eliminates the boundaries between indoor and outdoor space and creates an expansive effect. LED strip lights are hidden behind the valance trim throughout the interior and can be dimmed separately to create many different moods and vibrant environments. Like its namesake, Luna comes alive at night.

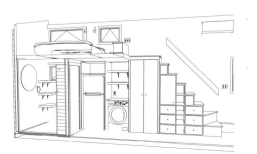

Storage and washing space

Luna Tiny Home

IMMERSO DIAMOND

Design:
Fabio Vignolio and Francesca Turnaturi

Location:
Alps, Italy

Job:
Build an experiential tourism cabin

Client:
Confidential

GFA:
6 m2

Completion:
2020

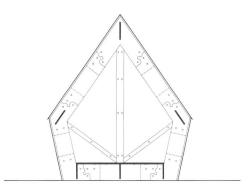

Immerso is a wooden prefabricated, temporary and contemporary shelter. The project envisualizes the increasing human need to live strictly connected to nature in manufactured form. It offers an opportunity to be immersed into nature in order to unplug from everyday routine and from the stress of urban life. People can observe the magnificence of landscapes around through the walls and from the roof of the accommodation and, during the night, they can admire the beauty of a starry sky. The goal is to test a new type of hospitality; as international trends like the glamping phenomenon show, Immerso offers an original experience linked to nature, supported by the research of details that pay attention to sustainability and respect for the environment.

QUATRO

Design:
Land Ark RV

Location:
Rifle, Colorado, USA

Job:
Design a mobile sleep and work dwelling

Client:
Confidential

GFA:
17.8 m2

Completion:
2022

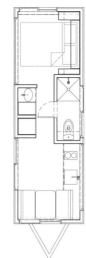

Floor plan

At 7.3 meter long, Quatro is the smallest Land Ark building to date. It derives its name from the four degree angles to the 2.4 meter wide windows in both the kitchen and bedroom. The living and kitchen area is ideal for dining, working or relaxing, and the banquette easily converts to a twin sleeper for an overnight guest. Down the hall is a split bathroom with a private shower and toilet room on one side, and a vanity on the other. When open, the pivoting bathroom door can latch across the hallway to turn the bedroom and bathroom into a suite with privacy from the living and kitchen. The ceiling height rises further to over 2.7 meters, as the bed easily folds up or down for added functionality.

VACATION HOME AHMEN FARM

Design:
Atelier Sunder-Plassmann

Location:
Kappeln, Germany

Job:
Build a vacation home as a lookout to nature

Client:
Ahmen farm

GFA:
55 m2

Completion:
2021

Ahmen farm, where the vacation home is located, is a rectangular farmstead surrounded by a large green area. The aim of the cottage is that the inhabitant becomes an observer of nature. Therefore this vacation home is completely glazed, blurring the boundaries between inside and outside. The visitor enters the cottage through a terrace, which serves as an outdoor area and an extension of the interior space in summer. The main room is subtly divided into three areas by an adjusted wall element, without dividing the space in its entirety. In front of the adjusted wall unit floats the kitchen. In the fully glazed cottage two wooden cubes are inserted, which accommodate the bunks. This closed volume forms a place of retreat in contrast to the open main room and conveys a feeling of security.

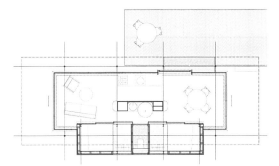

Floor plan

MAIDLA NATURE VILLA KASEKE

Design:
Mari Hunt and b210 architects

Location:
Rapla county, Estonia

Job:
Create a tiny house / hotel room

Client:
Maidla Nature Resort

GFA:
18 m2

Completion:
2020

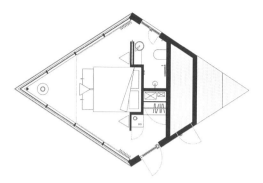

Floor plan

Maidla Nature Villa Kaseke

Inspired by wild nature, this building is nothing like a regular hotel room. The entire house is covered with terraces and is intended for one to two visitors at a time. The sharp angles of the building's triangular shapes blend into the surrounding bogland forest, due to its dark brown ash walls. Inside there is a fireplace, a bedroom and a separate work or rest area with small sofas. The triangular bedroom, facing wild nature, provides panoramic views of the scenic bogscape. A small bathroom includes floor-to-ceiling mirrors and an incineration toilet. All used materials are locally-sourced as much as possible. The interior of the tiny hotel is meticulously considered in the same style as the exterior – with the goal to blend in with nature, offer comfort and quality in materials.

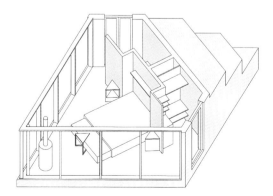

Isometry

Maidla Nature Villa Kaseke

LEVITZ MURPHY KITHAUS

Design:
KitHaus

Location:
Altadena, California, USA

Job:
Create an architectural accessory dwelling unit behind a mid century modern home

Client:
Brian Levitz and Randall Murphy

GFA:
37 m2

Completion:
2021

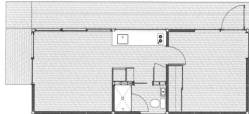

Floor plan

The modern residential unit was created to complement an existing mid-century home in Altadena, California. This KitHaus is nestled on a wooded lot in the foothills of the San Gabriel Mountains. The client wanted the structure to be integrated seamlessly into their backyard. A proprietary clear anodized aluminum framing along with Corten steel cladding and ipe hardwood siding helped integrate the module into the property. The architects provided custom glazing along with an individual maple plywood interior cladding with nickel trim.

FLOKE-HYTTENE

Design:
Holon Architecture

Location:
Ryvarden, Norway

Job:
Build a tiny holiday home with view to the sea

Client:
Haugesund Turistforening

GFA:
41 m2

Completion:
2020

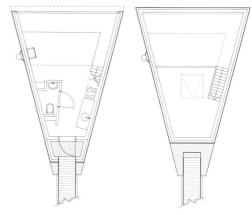

Ground and first floor plan

Situated on the far end of the headland in Sveio, a 30 minute drive from Haugesund, where endless sky meets the majestic sea, you can find the Ryvarden lighthouse. One of the major aspects for the project was that the cabins should not leave a permanent trace in the landscape. Four holes for each cabin, drilled in the rock to anchor the steel columns, is the only trace. There were no digging or leveling, and the end result is five cabins planned with the site in mind and with panoramic view over the North Sea. Their triangular shape and flat cut is chosen to withstand the strong winds at the Western Norwegian coast. They are all equipped with a kitchen, living room and a toilet. The heart of each cabin is a fireplace that allows guests to keep warm inside while watching the waves outside.

Flokehyttene

THE
TRAHAN

Design:
Fritz Tiny Homes

Location:
Vancouver Island, BC Canada

Job:
Provide a tiny home with micro gym and space
for yoga

Client:
Ashleigh Trahan

GFA:
33.6 m2

Completion:
2021

Tiny Living Spaces

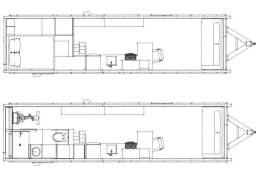

Loft and main floor plan

The Trahan

The Trahan is a fully equipped small house that optimizes the health and wellness of its users. It combines the style of an A-frame cottage with a mid-century modern mansion. At the left front of the home is a bright A-frame window with a curved 3.5 meter ceiling height and a luxurious green velvet couch. The right side features the loft, micro-gym, bathroom and laundry room in the back of the house. The living room can also be used as a yoga studio or an additional sleeping and dining area. Custom storage drawers under the couch incorporate a fold-out table and chairs. The Trahan also features a bright white kitchen, custom walnut cabinets, and stunning concrete countertops. Here, the designers made sure to keep everything away from the high walls and keep the functional space low.

THE SANNA HUT

Design:
Echo Living

Location:
Sanna, United Kingdom

Job:
Design and build a bespoke, sustainable cabin

Client:
G. & P. Crerar, Sanna

GFA:
29 m2

Completion:
2022

The Sanna Hut exemplifies Echo's aim to build small, build smart, and build beautiful. Its unique form is inspired by the remote Scottish coastal site, and is articulated in three elements, the largest reminiscent of a boat washed up on the foreshore, left balancing on a stony outcrop by the receding tide. Construction details that make use of innovative, sustainable materials are concealed within the sculptural form, which opens up to reveal a timber-lined, contemporary interior. Floor to ceiling windows offer panoramic views of the landscape, allowing daylight to spill into every corner of the space.

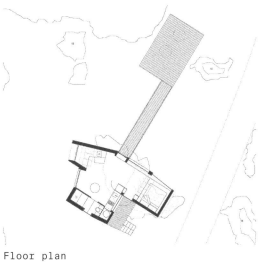

Floor plan

The Sanna Hut

NORWEGIAN BATHHOUSE

Design:
Handegård Arkitektur

Location:
Gressvik, Norway

Job:
Rebuild a bathhouse

Client:
Confidential

GFA:
18 m2

Completion:
2021

The Norwegian Bathhouse merges the traditional design of Norwegian bathhouses with modern building techniques. At first look, the bathhouse with its red-painted cladding and tin roof reminds of a traditional Norwegian boathouse. At a closer look, the angled cladding boards catch the eye. This modern take on the traditional building technique creates a semi-open space. The angled boards close the building towards the back and open it towards the front. This gives the bathhouse the feeling of a sheltering room at the same time as it enables a view over the entire sea. The building is designed with the thought of fitting into the environment. This is achieved by working with scarce details like the angled panels, instead of plain surfaces. The modern twist of the traditional Norwegian style is supported by the granite columns the house rests on.

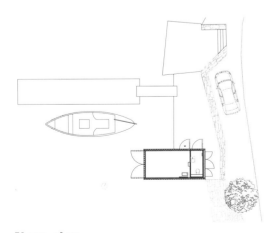

Floor plan

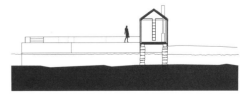

Section

Norwegian Bathhouse

WIKIHOUSE PETIT PLACE

Design:
RoosRos Architecten

Location:
Kader Zwijndrecht, The Netherlands

Job:
Build a fully modular and sustainable tiny house

Client:
ISA Beheer

GFA
40 m2

Completion:
2018

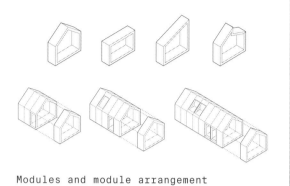

Modules and module arrangement

Petit Place is a tiny house which is fully modular and sustainable built. In addition to the spatial experience provided by the location, health and comfort are important design principles for this build. Petit Place is a construction kit with milled, wooden elements; an open-source solution which is accessible to everybody. The number of elements determines the size of the house. The building is divided into habitable zones thanks to the strategic positioning of the elements. The framework is completely circular. The exterior features solar panels which generate approximately 9,000 kWh per year. Other examples of cladding are called Green Machine, a fully planted version, and the so-called Zero Waste which has been created using reclaimed wood.

Floor plan

FREEDOMEK NR. 13

Design:
Freedomky

Location:
Zlin, Czech Republic

Job:
Build a man cave to relax and pursue hobbies

Client:
Confidential

GFA:
40 m2

Completion:
2013

Floor plan

Freedomek Nr. 13

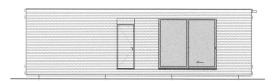

Front elevation

With the Freedomek, the dream of an own space can be fulfilled without a long building phase. The house is built in a hall, loaded onto a truck and taken anywhere the owner wants it to be. There is also an independent version of the Freedomek, with its own photovoltaic power plant, solar panels for hot water supply, wood stove, and wastewater treatment plant. The already spacious tiny house also has a three-meter folding terrace. The interior has a total floor area of 40 square meters and consists of a living room with a kitchenette, a bedroom, a bathroom with a toilet. Freedomek consists of 95 percent wood. The supporting structure is made of wood, dovetail joints, providing enormous strength and is insulated with wood-fiber board with great day-night phase shift. The façade is made of Nordic Larch.

INDEX

PICTURE CREDITS

IMPRINT

The Deutsche Nationalbibliothek lists
this publication in the Deutsche
Nationalbibliografie; detailed
bibliographic data are available on the
Internet at http://dnb.dnb.de

ISBN 978-3-03768-283-8

© 2023 by Braun Publishing AG
www.braun-publishing.ch

1st edition 2023

All of the information in this volume
has been compiled to the best of the
editor's knowledge. It is based on the
information provided to the publisher
by the architects' and designers'
offices and excludes any liability. The
publisher assumes no responsibility for
its accuracy or completeness as well as
copyright discrepancies and refers to
the specified sources (architects' and
designers' offices). All rights to the
photographs are property of the photo-
grapher (please refer to the picture
credits).

Editor:
Editorial Office van Uffelen

Editorial staff and layout:
Lara Stoller, Dorian van Uffelen,
Jacqueline Wenger

Graphic concept:
Edwin van Gelder, Mainstudio

Reproduction:
Bild1Druck GmbH, Berlin